The Politickle Pickle

Shreyas Navare freelances as editorial cartoonist, *Hindustan Times*. An MBA from IIT Bombay and a B.E. (IT) from VJTI, he is an ex-banker with five years of experience in marketing and technology. On behalf of *HT*, Shreyas has covered elections in six Indian states and presidential polls in the US. His works have been exhibited in India and abroad.

Praise for Shreyas Navare

'Keep it up! You show great promise.'—R.K. Laxman

'Navare's cartoons and caricatures have always managed to light up the pages of *Hindustan Times* as he uses wit and his unique style to comment on politics, business and society at large. His cartoons, which display a keen understanding of current affairs, sprinkled with the right dosage of levity, are a nice complement to our written pieces.'
—Sanjoy Narayan, Editor-in-Chief, *Hindustan Times*

'A cartoonist is an endangered species, which is why Shreyas Navare and his tribe need all our support. Shreyas's cartoons are a reminder that the art of satire is still an indispensable part of modern journalism. More power to him!'
—Rajdeep Sardesai, Editor-in-Chief, IBN18 Network

'The cartoons of Shreyas Navare are full of wit and wisdom. They carry important messages in a most enjoyable manner. I am glad they have been published in this book.'
—Prof M.S. Swaminathan, Father of India's Green Revolution

The Politickle Pickle

Shreyas Navare

Collins

First published in India in 2013 by Collins
An imprint of *HarperCollins Publishers* India

The cartoons and caricatures in this book have first appeared in the *Hindustan Times* (newspaper/website). Grateful acknowledgement is made to the *Hindustan Times* for permission to reproduce these cartoons and caricatures.

ISBN: 978-93-5116-095-3

2 4 6 8 10 9 7 5 3

Shreyas Navare asserts the moral right
to be identified as the author of this work.

HarperCollins *Publishers*
A-53, Sector 57, Noida, Uttar Pradesh 201301, India
77-85 Fulham Palace Road, London W6 8JB, United Kingdom
Hazelton Lanes, 55 Avenue Road, Suite 2900, Toronto, Ontario M5R 3L2
and 1995 Markham Road, Scarborough, Ontario M1B 5M8, Canada
25 Ryde Road, Pymble, Sydney, NSW 2073, Australia
31 View Road, Glenfield, Auckland 10, New Zealand
10 East 53rd Street, New York NY 10022, USA

Printed and bound at
Replika Press Pvt. Ltd.

To
Aaji, Mom, Dad and my sister

A.P.J. ABDUL KALAM

Art is an expression of the innate beauty in nature. Be it cartoon, sculpture or literary composition, art elevates the beautiful spirit of life for everyone to see and enjoy. It silently but eloquently conveys the message of love, humour, affection and peace.

The aim of the cartoonist is to elevate the soul of the reader and convey a difficult thought in such a way that the reader can laugh. My friend Shreyas Navare of the *Hindustan Times* does just that with his caricatures and cartoons, which make profound comments on the personalities and situations in our politics. This enables the reader to enjoy even the most difficult and complex situation. I congratulate Shreyas for his creativity. This collection of cartoons unravells the beauty of life in its noblest form. It enables us to reach for a higher, better and more civilized plane while imparting meaning and depth to our existence and justifying and vindicating the purpose of life. What more can you ask for, what more can you look for in a strife-stricken world where eternal human values are being mercilessly trampled upon and the beauty of life is lost in relentless materialistic pursuits?

While every cartoon of Shreyas makes the reader smile, I must mention a unique cartoon which I happened to see on Gandhi Jayanti, 2 October 2009. It was a panel titled 'Bapu's Visit'. In this, the father of the nation wakes up to the sound of violence around him. The next panel makes a comment on the typical problems the nation faces. On one side Mahatma Gandhi sees violence and on the other he witnesses the problems faced in the development schemes. In the next scene, President Obama is shown having a dream dinner with Gandhiji, with military actions in multiple theatres being planned in the background. The only beautiful thing Gandhiji sees is a girl child sitting outside her hut and studying with the help of lights emanating from the malls on the opposite side of the road. This brings tears in Mahatma Gandhi's eyes as he sees the child saying, 'Hum Honge Kamyaab Ek Din.' People miss the Mahatma. What a beautiful thought this cartoon of Shreyas puts forth. Pain is followed by the hope the young generation brings to our nation.

Although all men are created equal, some consciously develop their faculties to such magnificent proportions that they come to be known as the 'gifted lot'. I have always had a tremendous fascination for them. Cartoonists do occupy a pride of place in our society for bringing cheer to readers. There is a message in every cartoon, delivered with tremendous humour and without any rancour. In a few line sketches, Shreyas captures the soul of the nation, its agony, its joy and also gives pointers to our future. He pours his genius into the works of art for us to see, feel and understand what India stands for or ought to stand for. This work, I am sure, will inspire people of our country, particularly the youth, and motivate them to lead better lives while smiling at our own follies.

(Excerpts from inaugural address at Shreyas Navare's cartoon exhibition in Bengaluru on 10 January 2010)

Indrajit Hazra

I know this is a rather strange thing to say, but unlike political writers – and most certainly unlike the political animals who take the centre stage – political cartoonists are usually a quiet bunch.

One would have thought that with their unique talent for capturing lightnings in bottles, cartoonists dealing with the phlegm-clearing world of politics would be a raucous lot. And yet having had the pleasure of chatting with visual-textual commentators of the class of R.K. Laxman and Chandi Lahiri (the Bengali cartoonist of my generation) and from what I've read and heard about others, political and social cartoonists of a certain calibre are a quiet bunch – the late Balasaheb Thackeray being a notable exception.

This quality also holds for another favourite political cartoonist of mine: Shreyas Navare. When I first got in touch with Shreyas over email in 2007, going by the samples of his works that I had seen, I remember mistaking his enthusiasm for qualities of the proverbial Angry Young Man. But when I met him face to face in the *Hindustan Times*' Mumbai office in Mahim a few months later in 2008, the young man in front of me was a soft-spoken IIT Mumbai graduate who had just started his first job in a bank.

Perhaps there is some logic in this cartoonist paradox. Shreyas's works are indeed sprinkled with a certain kind of anger, an anger that comes out of being aghast at various moments of the running tragic-comedy that is Indian politics. But this anger somehow changes into rapier wit and, on many occasions, even into full-blown slapstick comedy.

Whether it be his multiple takes on Rahul Baba's perpetual Prince Charles-like 'preparedness' as India's prime minister, or his opinion on the ridiculousness of various aspects of coalition politics, or his depiction of the litany of scandals that come with seasonal regularity and increasing size, Shreyas's cartoons in the *Hindustan Times* since late 2007 have captured more than just the spirit of our times. They have also mirrored their absurdities.

I believe that 'Big Deal', Shreyas's cartoon commentary which has been running every Saturday in the *Hindustan Times* since 2008, not only brings pleasure and an awareness of what a political event means, but it also reminds us that there is a particular kind of tool that we not only can use, but must use as members of society: criticism that can shame and embarrass.

And this is where Shreyas the quiet, soft-spoken cartoonist, with his vibrant, almost childish Disney colourings held together by bold scrawl lines depicting Manmohan Singh, Narendra Modi, Salman Khurshid, Anna Hazare, Madonna and son Gandhis – the whole roster of characters that Indian politics throws up like a confetti machine – shows courage without which no political cartoonist can survive from his own notions of politeness and propriety.

One of the best things in my stint as editor of the *Hindustan Times*' Comment section has been to find Shreyas a platform from which to give his sharp, comic, trenchant commentary every Saturday. For this, I will unashamedly pat myself on the back. But Shreyas deserves much more and this will become obvious to those turning the pages of the book that you now hold. Being one of contemporary India's finest political cartoonists is a very big deal.

(Indrajit Hazra is a novelist and journalist. He is the former editor of the Comment section of *Hindustan Times* where he is currently consultant editor)

Shreyas Navare

FOR BIHAR

FOR INDIA

Shreyas Navare

8

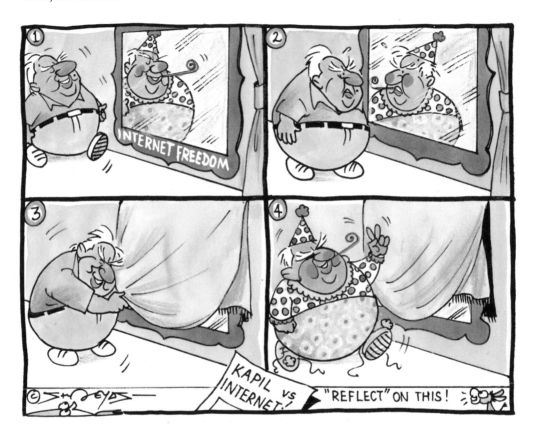

The Politickle Pickle

NAMO IN 3-D!

CM 2012

PM 2014

GUJ POLLS!

3-Ds: DELHI, DELHI, DELHI?

15

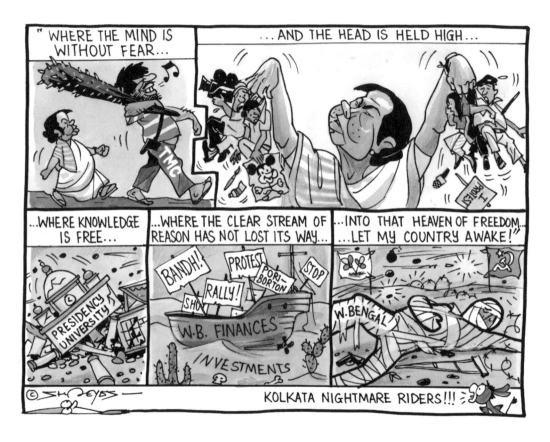

Shreyas Navare

Shreyas Navare

The Politickle Pickle

Shreyas Navare

Shreyas Navare

BAL THACKERAY
1926-2012

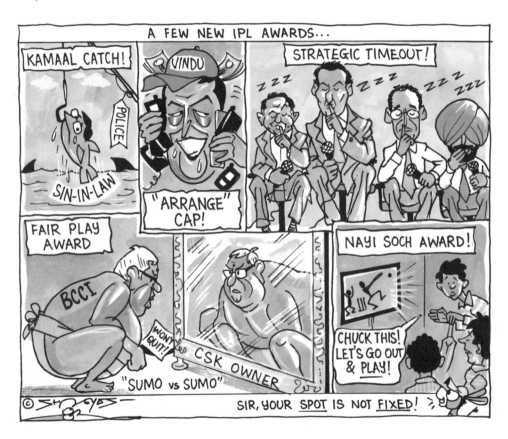

43

Shreyas Navare

Shreyas Navare

Shreyas Navare

Shreyas Navare

Shreyas Navare

The Politickle Pickle

61

Shreyas Navare

64

Shreyas Navare

Shreyas Navare

68

Shreyas Navare

INDIA'S "DISCOVERY OF RAHUL" !!

77

Shreyas Navare

The Politickle Pickle

79

Shreyas Navare

Shreyas Navare

Shreyas Navare

Shreyas Navare

Shreyas Navare

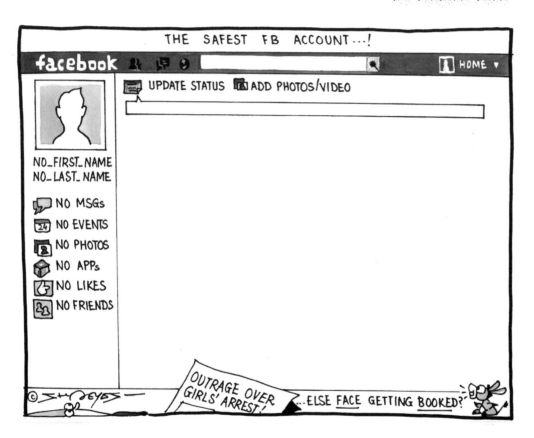

Shreyas Navare

Shreyas Navare

The Politickle Pickle

107

Shreyas Navare

Shreyas Navare

The Politickle Pickle

119

Shreyas Navare

Shreyas Navare

Shreyas Navare

Shreyas Navare

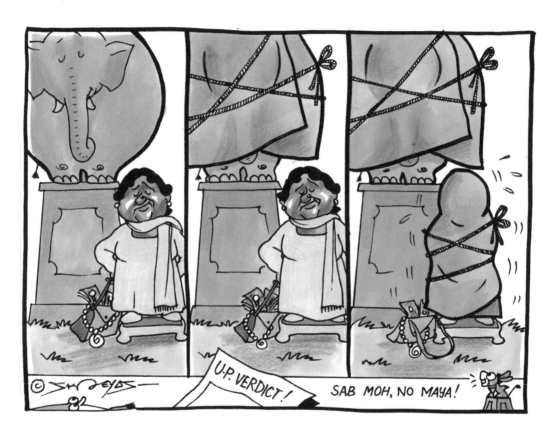

Shreyas Navare

Shreyas Navare

138

Shreyas Navare

Shreyas Navare

Shreyas Navare

146

Shreyas Navare

Shreyas Navare

Shreyas Navare

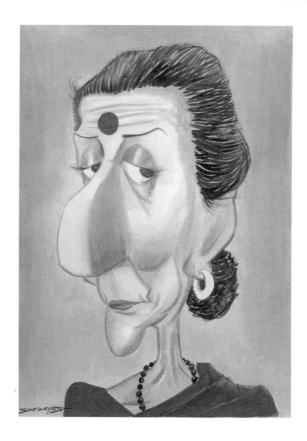

Shreyas Navare

Shreyas Navare

Shreyas Navare

Shreyas Navare

164

Shreyas Navare

166

Shreyas Navare

Shreyas Navare

Shreyas Navare

Shreyas Navare

Shreyas Navare

Shreyas Navare

The Politickle Pickle

187

Shreyas Navare

ACKNOWLEDGEMENTS

I am deeply grateful to Dr A.P.J. Abdul Kalam, Mr R.K. Laxman and Mrs Kamala Laxman for their blessings and constant encouragement for my cartooning since my student days. I feel honoured and humbled that these great personalities have contributed the foreword and the lead testimonial for this book.

My heartfelt gratitude to Shantanu Ray Chaudhuri of HarperCollins for his invaluable contribution, guidance and support in bringing this book to life; to Sanjoy Narayan for the faith reposed in me by *Hindustan Times* and for penning his kind words about the cartoons; to Indrajit Hazra for providing a wonderful platform for my cartoons in the *Hindustan Times* and for contributing the generous introduction; to Shuka Jain and Arijit Ganguly for their insightful inputs for the cover design; to Rajatveer Singh Yadav for designing the book layout and typesetting the book in a very short time; to Prof. M.S. Swaminathan and Rajdeep Sardesai for their kind encouragement through testimonials; to Usha Laxman, R.K. Prasad, Soumya Bhattacharya, Parveen Gupta and Renuka Narayanan for their guidance, advice and help since the earliest days of this project; to Neelu Prabhakar and Girija Padmanabhan for their unstinted support; to Prof. Anita Sharan and Samar Halarnkar for initiating my journey at *Hindustan Times*; to my alma maters, IIT Bombay and VJTI, for playing hosts to my earliest cartoon exhibitions; to my previous organizations, Yes Bank and Tata Consultancy Services, for their out-of-the-way encouragement and support for my cartooning; to my teachers and friends from Smt. Sulochanadevi Singhania School, for not minding being the earliest targets of a cartoonist's brush; and to my family for being the bedrock of my life.